P9-DTE-608

GARNISHING

GARNISHING

STEP-BY-STEP INSTRUCTIONS IN THE ART OF PREPARING GORGEOUS FOOD

DR. OETKER

Translated from the German by
John M. Kleeberg and adapted for the
American kitchen by Lois Hill

WEATHERVANE BOOKS
NEW YORK

First published in Germany under the title
Garnieren, Verzieren, Dekorieren.

Copyright © 1987 by Ceres-Verlag, R.A. Oetker KG
Bielefeld, Federal Republic of Germany

Translation copyright © 1989 by OBC, Inc.
All rights reserved.

This 1989 edition is published by Weathervane
Books, distributed by Crown Publishers, Inc.,
225 Park Avenue South, New York, New York 10003,
by arrangement with Ceres-Verlag R.A.

Printed and Bound in the United States of America

Library of Congress Cataloging-in-Publication Data

Garnieren, verzieren, dekorieren. English.
    Garnishing : step-by-step instructions in the art of
preparing gorgeous food / Dr. Oetker : translated by John M.
Kleeberg and edited by Lois Hill.
        p.   cm.
    Translation of: Garnieren, verzieren, dekorieren.
    ISBN 0-517-68792-5
    1. Cookery (Garnishes)   2. Cookery (Cold dishes)
3. Desserts.   4. Table setting and decoration.   I. Dr. Oetker
(Firm)   II. Title.
TX652.G3613   1989
641.5—dc19   89-5641
                                                    CIP

h g f e d c b a

CONTENTS

FOREWORD

Everyone admires a professionally catered buffet table, with its lovely centerpiece, elegantly garnished platters of hot and cold food, and beautifully decorated desserts. Now, with the easy-to-follow, step-by-step instructions in this book you will see how easy it is to add professional touches to the food you serve in your own home.

In addition to teaching new garnishing and decorating techniques, *Garnishing* offers many exciting ideas for the presentation of fruit, vegetables, and desserts as well as meat, poultry, fish, cheese, and salads. Every technique is described with step-by-step, full-color photographs. There are also many suggestions for food presentation that you can adapt when serving your own favorite dishes. These techniques for elegantly preparing and presenting food require no additional expenditure. You probably already have most of the necessary utensils in your own kitchen.

Whether you entertain on a grand or an intimate scale, *Garnishing* will help you add a very special touch to every dish.

1. Wire rack
2./3./4./5. Hearts, stars, diamond-shaped
and scallop-edged cookie cutters
6. Dough comb
7. Pastry brushes
8. Vegetable peeler

9. Melon baller
10. Oval melon baller
11. Lemon zester
12. Corer

UTENSILS

13. Grooved knife
14. Egg separator
15. Egg slicer
16. Tips for pastry tubes
17. Baking parchment cone

18. Pastry tube with tip
19. Double-handled chopper
21. Ridged knife
20./22./23. Assorted kitchen knives

PINEAPPLE

Pineapple makes an elegant dessert at any time of the year. For each serving, halve two slices of pineapple from which the core has been removed. Arrange them around a whole, cored pineapple slice on attractive plates, as in the illustration above. Roll thinly sliced pieces of pineapple into rosettes and arrange in the pineapple ring. Garnish with seedless green grapes and mint leaves. Top each rosette with a raspberry. Just before serving, add a light dusting of confectioner's sugar.

Garnishing suggestions using pineapple, grapes, and tangerine segments are shown on the facing page. They can be used to decorate buffet platters, puddings, or cakes. Instructions for making these and other garnishes are given on pages 14 and 15.

The pineapple boat with shrimp makes a light and attractive appetizer.
Pineapple, tangerine, and grape kebabs can be served with drinks or to decorate a platter of canapes.
You can also use the various pineapple motifs shown to garnish ice cream, puddings, and custards.

To make pineapple rosettes, peel the pineapple and cut off several slices. Remove the hard inner core.

Use a very sharp knife to cut the pineapple into a thin strip. Roll into a rosette, and insert in the pineapple ring.

To make a pineapple boat, cut an unpeeled pineapple into halves and then into quarters. Then cut the fruit from the rind.

Slice the pineapple and arrange the slices in the rind.

Garnishing Suggestions

Arrange quartered pineapple slices in a row or, perhaps, around a platter. Garnish every slice with a strawberry half and small mint leaves.

Arrange pineapple wedges and cherries, alternating the fruits as shown above.

Add a rosette of whipped cream to the center of a slice of pineapple. Decorate with a piece of chocolate and pistachio nuts.

When you cut a pineapple into slices, cookie or biscuit cutters can be used to trim off the rind and remove the hard core.

Grapes and tiny tangerine segments can be used to garnish pineapple rings. Make a cut three-quarters of the way down in large green and black grapes and embellish as shown with grape slices and tangerine segments.

APPLES AND PEARS

To make the attractive apple dessert illustrated above, peel 2 apples, but leave the stems attached. Marinate the apples in 1 cup of red wine for 25 minutes, turning the fruit frequently. Halve the apples and remove the cores. Prepare a cherry-flavored or mixed fruit packaged gelatin according to the instructions on the box, but substitute ½ cup of white wine for ½ cup of the water heated to dissolve the gelatin. Spoon a little of the gelatin into the apple halves. Cover the bottom of four dessert plates or shallow soup bowls with the remaining gelatin. Place the filled apple halves in the middle of the plate and refrigerate for at least 2 hours. When the gelatin has set, decorate with apple slices, quartered pistachios, and red currants; add rosettes of whipped cream. This is a delicious and original dessert.

Garnishing suggestions using apples and pears are shown on the facing page.

Apples and pears can be marinated in red wine and served with meat dishes. They also make elegant desserts with a vanilla or chocolate sauce.
Marinated, cored pear slices and halves can be shaped with a cookie cutter and decorated with kiwis, strawberries, and grapes. Instructions for making these garnishes are given on pages 18 and 19.

An apple slicer, which divides an apple into neat equal parts, and cores it at the same time, is a useful gadget.

To make the pear "fan" shown on page 16, peel a pear, but leave the stem attached. Marinate in ½ cup of red wine for 25 minutes, turning the pear frequently. Slice the pear in half. Using a sharp knife, cut the pear from stem to bottom and arrange the pieces in the shape of a fan.

To make apple slices, peel an apple and marinate in ½ cup of white wine for 25 minutes, turning it frequently. Slice the apple and use a small cookie or biscuit cutter to remove the core.

Remove the outer edge of the cored apple slice with a scallop-edged cookie cutter. Garnish the apple slices with strawberry halves, kiwi slices, and grape quarters.

To make the attractive apple garnish shown on page 16, first cut a quarter out of an apple.

Lay the apple quarter on its side. Using a sharp knife, carefully cut the center from the quarter, working from both sides into the middle.

Repeat the process with the remaining piece. Rub lemon juice on the cut surfaces of the apple to prevent it from browning.

Arrange the apple slices as shown.

EXOTIC FRUIT

To make the beautiful fruit plate shown above, peel a kiwi and cut it into slices. Arrange the slices on an attractive plate. Decorate with thin strips of papaya, drained canned litchis, candied orange peel, and a fresh basil leaf.

Garnishing suggestions using exotic fruit are shown on the facing page.

Cut the top off a grapefruit or a pomelo to create a zigzag pattern. Decorate with strips of papaya and kiwi, lemon quarters, and small flowers.
Halve and peel a persimmon. Decorate with pieces cut from the other half of the persimmon and embellish with a rosette of whipped cream.
Halve a mango. Cut out the pit. Fill the mango half with slices and balls prepared from the remaining half.
Kumquats, peeled litchis, grapefruit sections, persimmons, and kiwi slices may be used to garnish both sweet and spicy dishes.

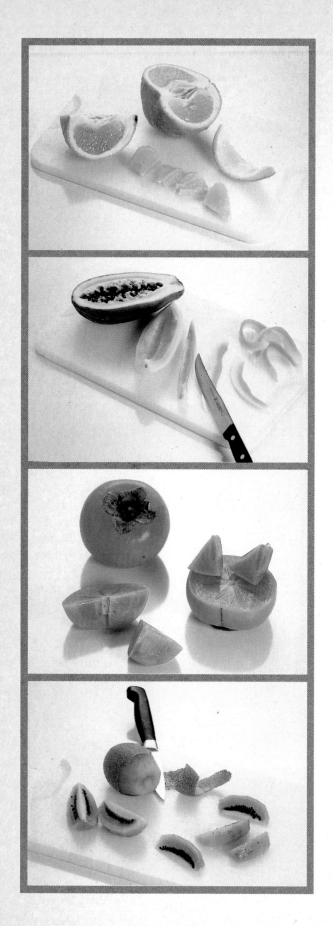

Pomelo is a citrus fruit that comes from Israel. It has a fresh, slightly bitter taste. Grapefruit is an excellent substitute for pomelo.
Garnishing idea: Halve and quarter a pomelo. Separate the fruit from the rind and cut into slices. Use pomelo slices to decorate puddings or cold souffles.

Papaya is grown in South America, Asia, and Africa; it has a light, sweet flavor.
Garnishing idea: Halve a papaya lengthwise and cut off the skin. Scrape out the seeds with a spoon. Cut the fruit into strips. Use papaya strips to decorate desserts.

The persimmon originates in East Asia. It has a very soft, sweet flesh. Never use a persimmon before it is soft and fully ripened.
Garnishing idea: Halve a persimmon crosswise. Cut into quarters, then into eighths. Remove the seeds. Serve with ice cream.

Kiwi comes from New Zealand, but is now grown in California. This pale green, soft fruit has a slightly sour, grapelike flavor.
Garnishing idea: Peel a kiwi, divide into halves, and then into eighths. Cut out the white inner core. Use kiwis slices to decorate desserts, and buffet platters.

Mangos grow in East Asia, Africa, South America, Florida, and Israel. An extremely soft and somewhat pulpy fruit, mango tastes much like a peach.
Garnishing idea: Cut a mango lengthwise. Cut out the pit and slice the fruit into strips. Serve with appetizers and desserts.

The kumquat grows in East Asia, Africa, and the United States. Kumquats may be eaten unpeeled. Cut into decorative strips, a kumquat makes an attractive garnish for poultry, cheese, or meat.

The litchi nut comes from China or Africa. Litchis have a slightly sour taste that has been compared to cherries. In the West, fresh litchis are rarely available, but canned, pitted litchis have good flavor and texture.
Garnishing idea: Drain canned litchis. Fill with rosettes of whipped cream. Use litchis to embellish desserts.

The karambola, or star fruit, originates in Thailand. Its sweet-and-sour taste is reminiscent of quince and gooseberries.
Garnishing idea: Slice a star fruit. Use these naturally star-shaped slices to decorate desserts and buffet platters.

CITRUS FRUIT

Cut a lemon in half. With a sharp paring knife, trim a thin strip from the peel, but do not cut it off. Wrap the strip once around the lemon and use it to decorate the top of the lemon half.

Use a grooved knife to cut even channels lengthwise in a lemon. Then cut the lemon into slices.

Make eight cuts in a lemon from the top almost to the bottom. Gently pull it partially apart. Place thin lime wedges in the openings.

Cut a lime into slices. Make a small cut in the middle of each slice and twist the slices into spirals.

Cut a grapefruit in half. Cut grooves in the peel with an oval melon baller.

To make an orange basket, cut into the orange twice from the top to the middle to create the handle. Then make zigzag cuts around the middle. Remove the pulp from the handle.

Remove strips from the peel of a lemon or an orange with a lemon zester and use to decorate a lemon slice.

With a sharp paring knife, make a zigzag cut into the middle of a lemon. Pull the two halves apart and then put them back together as shown.

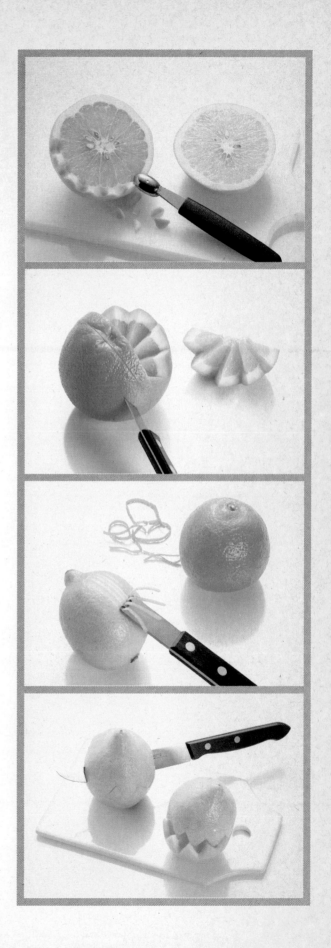

Using a sharp paring knife, peel an orange so the rind and pith are removed in one continuous strip.

Cut the orange into sections.

Instructions for making the decorations shown on pages 28 and 29:

Make ten cuts in a tangerine from the top to the bottom as shown. Pull out every other section of the peel and decorate with mint leaves.
Halve an orange and decorate with orange sections and halved red grapes.
Using a grooved knife, cut the peel of an orange or tangerine into slanting strips from top to bottom.
Peel an orange rind in one thin strip and arrange in an attractive design.
Make eight cuts in an orange from top to bottom and remove the fruit. Arrange the strips of peel into a star. In the center of the star arrange orange slices and top with mint leaves. Alternate orange slices, scallop-edged lemon slices (use a channel knife), and kiwi slices.

Garnishing suggestions for oranges and tangerines are shown on the facing page.

Tangerine sections (with the membranes removed) and fresh basil leaves arranged in the shape of a star.
A scallop-edged orange slice topped with lemon slices arranged in a spiral.
Peel a lemon and an orange. Cut the peels into attractive shapes.
Peel an orange in one thin, continuous strip and roll it into the shape of a rose.
All of these garnishing suggestions can be used to decorate platters of fish, meat, and poultry, as well as desserts.

MELONS AND FIGS

Melon and thinly sliced Parma ham is a delicious combination and makes an elegant appetizer, as illustrated above. Cut a honeydew melon into eighths. Cut the fruit from the rind. Arrange thin melon slices with slices of ham on the rind. Decorate with mint leaves.

Garnishing suggestions for melon and figs are shown opposite.

To make the melon boat shown on the facing page, first cut a melon into eighths. Using one of the wedges that you will not need to serve, cut out the fruit with a star-shaped cookie cutter. Use a toothpick to arrange a star on the melon wedge. Cut the top off a melon, remove the seeds, and scoop out some of the fruit. Fill the melon shell with melon balls of various types; decorate with fresh currants or raspberries.
Make a zigzag around the upper third of a melon and lift off the top. Decorate the melon sections as you wish. The photograph shows melons garnished with kiwis, ham slices, figs cut open in the shape of stars, melon balls, and grapes.

Instructions for making the decorations shown on pages 32 and 33:

Decorate a melon wedge with thin apple slices and a cherry.
Decorate a melon wedge with halved fresh figs and a mint leaf.
Remove the fruit from an eighth of a melon, cut into wedges, and put it back into the melon rind. Embellish with grapes, melon balls, and fresh sage leaves.
Halve several fresh figs and decorate with melon balls.

CUCUMBERS AND ZUCCHINI

To make the attractive dish shown above, prepare cucumber slices (see step 8, page 39) and arrange on an attractive plate. Using a cookie cutter, cut out star-shaped slices from a zucchini and use to decorate an obliquely cut piece of cucumber. Served with black bread and butter, this dish makes a simple appetizer or salad.

On the facing page there are a number of garnishing ideas using cucumbers, pickles, and zucchini. Instructions for making many of these are given on pages 38 and 39.

These garnishes can be used to decorate cheese platters, as well as platters of cold meat or hors d'oeuvres. Add sprigs of dill or small sage leaves.

To make a zucchini boat, cut off the bottom of a small zucchini so it will lie flat. Cut the ends off obliquely. Using a sharp paring knife, cut a thin, flat slice almost to the end of the top of the zucchini, and roll as shown. Cut two more slices, and roll them under as illustrated.

Cut three thin strips from half a yellow pepper from which the white pith has been removed. Place the pepper strips over the zucchini rolls. Use additional strips of pepper and fresh sage leaves to decorate the zucchini boat.

To make a pickle fan, cut a small pickle in half. Slice each half from the top almost to the bottom. Arrange the cut pickles to create fans.

To make an attractive garnish with zucchini, make zigzag cuts with a sharp paring knife on the top side of a thick slice of zucchini. Lightly press the top of the cut zucchini into curry powder or paprika.

To make an attractive garnish for a buffet platter, cut flower shapes from thin slices of cucumber using a scallop-edged cookie cutter. Press out the same shapes from sections of a yellow pepper from which the white pith has been removed. Arrange the cucumber rings and cucumber and pepper flowers in a decorative alternating pattern.

To make an attractive garnish, cut two fairly thick cucumber slices and two very thin cucumber slices. Slice into the middle of the thin cucumber slices and twist each one into a spiral. Arrange the spirals on the cucumber slices and garnish with sprigs of fresh dill.

For another cucumber decoration, use a sharp paring knife to cut one-third of the peel off three cucumber slices, making a zigzag pattern. Arrange the slices on top of each other, so they face in alternate directions as shown. Decorate with a curl of cucumber peel.

To make a cucumber spiral, use a long thin cucumber. Cut off the ends. Pierce the cucumber lengthwise with a wooden kebab stick. Using a sharp paring knife, cut slices all the way around the cucumber, but only in as far as the kebab stick. Remove the stick, being careful not to pull the pieces of cucumber apart, and arrange the cucumber into a spiral.

PEPPERS AND CELERY

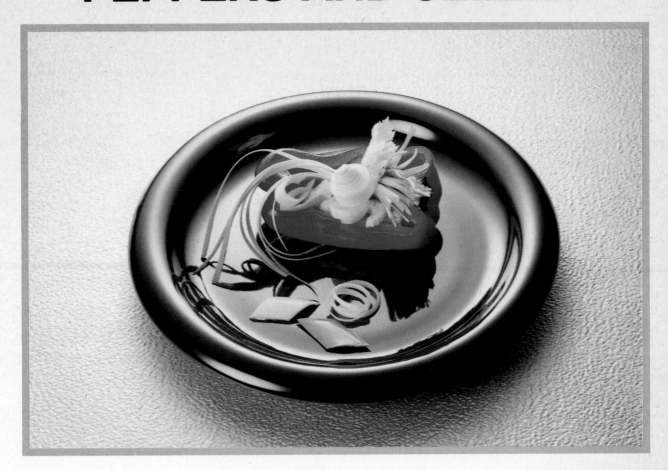

To make the attractive dish illustrated above, halve red peppers from which the seeds and white pith have been removed. Fill the pepper halves with thin strips of steamed leeks or fresh scallions and slices of celery. Arrange on a salad plate. This attractively garnished pepper can be served as an appetizer or salad with a vinaigrette or a herb dressing.

On the facing page there are many ideas for garnishes using peppers and celery.

To make the pepper boats, halve a red pepper crosswise and remove the seeds and white pith. Fill with diced celery, whole small mushrooms, and garnish with sprigs of fresh parsley and dill. Cut red, green, and yellow peppers into rings and link them as shown.
Using a ridged knife, cut celery stalks, which have been blanched, into diamond shapes, curly strips, and flowers. Decorate with pieces of pepper and rosettes of sour cream. Using a pastry tube with a star-shaped tip, embellish a celery stalk with rosettes of sour cream or cream cheese softened with cream. Cut sections of multi-colored peppers into strips, leaving a base of about 1 inch, and intertwine to create tassels.
Cut a red pepper into quarters, remove the seeds and white pith. Fill with swirls of sour cream or cream cheese.

CARROTS

Instructions for the garnishes illustrated above and on the facing page are provided on pages 44 and 45. Carrots make attractive, edible decorations for hot or cold buffet platters of vegetables and meat, fish, and poultry dishes.

On the facing page are carrot slices arranged into the shape of a flower. A scallion slice is used for the center.
Carrot letters or an entire carrot cut into a spiral make festive decorations for a children's party.
An alternating arrangement of cucumber and carrot slices is an easy, colorful garnish for a platter of cheese or sausage sandwiches.

Using a vegetable peeler, cut four thin slices in one side of a small carrot as shown. If the carrot is put into a bowl of ice-cold water in the refrigerator for several hours the slices will curl up.

With a grooved knife, make ridges in a scraped carrot from top to bottom. Cut the carrot into slices, cut the slices in halves, and arrange in an attractive pattern.

A large scraped carrot can be cut into a spiral using a sharp paring knife.

Slices of large, scraped carrot can be cut into assorted letters.

Use a ridged knife to slice a scraped carrot. Alternate the carrot slices with half slices of cucumber.

Use a vegetable peeler to make a miniature carrot. Use a toothpick to secure carrot greens or parsley sprigs to the top.

Use a julienne knife to cut thin strips from a carrot. Arrange the julienne strips on a leaf of endive.

To make a carrot flower, thinly slice a small, scraped carrot. Form the stem and leaves from a leek or scallion. Arrange the carrot slices around a small leek or scallion ring in the shape of a flower. Brush with dissolved unflavored gelatin to make the flower shine.

RED AND WHITE RADISHES

Imaginative and simple decorations can be achieved using radishes. Instructions for making the garnishes illustrated above and on the facing page are given on pages 48 and 49.

Small fresh sage leaves or small radish leaves add contrast to cut, carved, or peeled radishes. With their brilliant red coloring, radishes can be used as garnishes for cheese, meat, and fish platters, as well as for salads.

To make a radish flower, use a sharp paring knife to cut the peel off a radish from the top almost to the bottom at eight equal intervals. Put the radish in a bowl of ice-cold water. After several hours the radish will "blossom."

To make an attractive radish rosette, cut into the middle of a large radish from the top almost to the bottom at eight equal intervals. Gently pull slightly apart. Place thin radish slices in the openings as shown.

To carve a radish flower, use a sharp paring knife to cut wedges out of a radish at equal intervals as shown.

Make four semi-circular cuts into the radish peel above the stem, make another two cuts to form a cross. Place in a bowl of ice-cold water in the refrigerator for at least one hour.

The garnishing suggestions shown above are ideas for more decorations for large buffet platters or snacks. Instructions are given below.

Cut a thick slice of peeled white radish. Cut the white radish both lengthwise and cross-wise almost to the bottom. Insert half-slices of red radish and alfafa sprouts.

To make radish curls, use a sharp paring knife to cut thin strips from a peeled white radish.

TOMATOES AND ONIONS

Tomatoes and onions can be used to make exciting garnishes as well as baskets. Instructions to make some of the garnishes illustrated above and on the facing page are given on pages 52 and 53.

When using a tomato for decorative purposes it is sometimes advisable to peel it. To remove the skin from a tomato, put the tomato into a bowl. Pour boiling water into the bowl to cover the tomato. After 3 to 5 minutes drain the tomato and peel off the skin.

Tomatoes and onions are especially recommended for garnishing platters of meat and fish.

To create a tomato rose, use a sharp paring knife to peel the skin off the tomato. Roll the skin into a rose. Secure with a toothpick, if necessary.

To make an attractive, edible garnish, halve a tomato, slice it thinly at equal intervals almost to the other side, and insert small pieces of onion.

To make this large decoration, cut the top off a large tomato and turn it upside down. Make eight cuts halfway down at even intervals. Place the tomato in boiling water for 2 to 3 minutes, or until the skin loosens. Rinse in cold water. Using a sharp paring knife, carefully turn back the skin as shown.

Scoop out some of the tomato with a spoon. Decorate the tomato with onion rings and capers.

To create a tomato basket, make a zigzag cut around the center of a tomato with a sharp knife. Pull the halves apart. Use a spoon to hollow out the tomato. Fill with pearl onions.

To make an onion flower, cut a slice from a large, unpeeled onion. Separate some of the skin as shown. Top the onion slice with thin half-slices of a small red onion and flat parsley leaves.

To make an onion chrysanthemum, cut a peeled yellow or red onion almost to the middle at eight equal intervals. Refrigerate in a bowl of ice-water for 1 hour.

To make an onion flower, cut the core from a peeled onion that has been cut almost to the middle at equal intervals. Gently pull the segments slightly apart. Put a tomato slice in the center. Top with small onion rings and alfalfa sprouts.

53

SALAD PLATTER

POTATOES

Potato balls, slices of unpeeled new potatoes, and riced potatoes arranged on half a potato and garnished with tender young leaves of lamb's lettuce or arugula, as illustrated above, make attractive garnishes for platters of meat or vegetables.

On the facing page there are a number of garnishing ideas using potatoes. Instructions for making many of these appear on pages 58 and 59.

A potato cut into the shape of a basket and potato balls arranged on a leaf of curly lettuce can be used to decorate platters of meat. Potato rosettes make an attractive edible garnish.

To make potato balls, boil and peel a large potato. When the potato is cool, use a melon baller to cut out large balls.

To make a potato-stick basket, peel several large potatoes, cut them into thin julienne strips, and fry the strips in hot vegetable oil until half done—about 2 minutes. Remove from oil and let cool.

Arrange the potato strips in a basket shape in a sieve or strainer. Place a second sieve on top and deep-fry in hot oil, until the potato basket is brown and crisp—2 to 3 minutes.

To make a potato basket, peel and boil a medium-sized round potato. Use directions from earlier "basket." Cut out a small basket, remove the pieces between the handle and the basket, and decorate with fresh herbs.

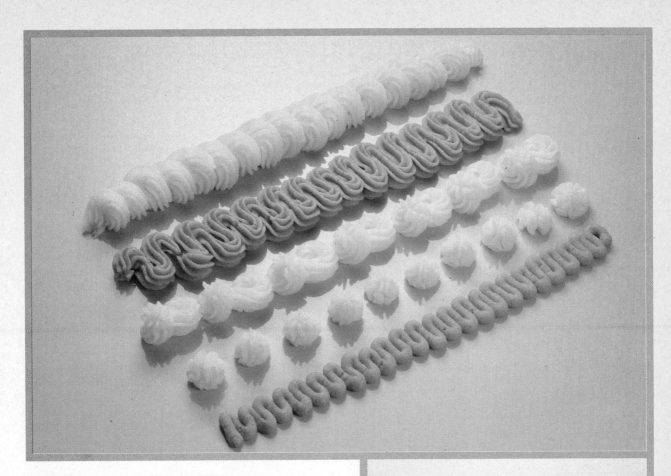

To make potato rosettes and borders, put mashed or pureed potatoes into a pastry tube. Use a smooth or grooved tip to create various shapes. Sweet potatoes or white potatoes can be used.

For attractive potato decorations, peel and boil a large potato. When the potato is cool, cut it into thin slices. Use small cookie cutters to make a variety of different shapes which can then be arranged on serving plates.

A simple garnish can be made by cutting slices of a peeled, boiled potato with a ridged knife.

Eggs seem to lend themselves to embellishment. Below are directions to make the garnishes.

To make elegant deviled eggs, illustrated on pages 60 and 61, cut a hard-boiled egg in half lengthwise. Remove the yolk and mix it with 1 tablespoon of mayonnaise. Using a pastry tube, pipe a yolk rosette into the one egg white half. Decorate with an olive slice and strips of egg white made from the other half.

To make the shrimp and egg canape, cut a hard-boiled egg in half crosswise. Remove the yolk. Drop a raw egg white into boiling water mixed with 1 tablespoon of wine vinegar. Remove with a slotted spoon. Arrange the cooked egg white with shrimp and chicory leaves in the egg half as shown.

To make a quail-egg appetizer, cook a raw egg white thoroughly in boiling water mixed with 1 tablespoon of wine vinegar. Arrange the cooked egg white with hard-boiled quail eggs on an endive leaf, and dust with paprika.

To make an olive and egg canape, cut a hard-boiled egg in half and remove the yolk. Fill the hollowed-out egg white half with sliced stuffed olives, and garnish with strips of egg white cut from the other half.

To make an egg flower, cut a hard-boiled egg into thin slices from the ends of the egg. Press out the petals using a tear-shaped cookie cutter. Form a flower using a center of egg yolk.

To make an egg and tomato mushroom, cut the ends off a hard-boiled egg. Place half a cherry tomato on top of the egg. Dot with mayonnaise as shown.

An attractive garnish can be made with tomato and egg wedges. Split a hard-boiled egg into wedges using an egg divider. Alternate the wedges with tomato wedges.

Eggs and smoked salmon make a lovely combination. Cut three slices from the center of a hard-boiled egg. Garnish with smoked salmon, strips of lemon peel, sprigs of fresh dill, and very thin, peeled lemon slices.

HERBS

Herbs can be used to dress up many dishes. The elegant herb flower above has a stem made of chive stalks, flowers from red radish slices, and leaves fashioned from dill.

The herb rosette, above, is made by mixing sour cream with chopped herbs. Use a pastry tube with a jagged tip and press the rosette directly onto the serving dish; decorate with fresh basil.

On the facing page there are a number of ideas for herb garnishes.

The herb wreath is made of a variety of fresh herbs such as parsley, sage, rosemary, dill, marjoram, and mint. The herbs are tied onto a thin wire to form a wreath, which will keep for about one day when placed in water or in a plastic bag in the refrigerator. Surrounding a dish filled with sour cream dip or herb butter, the wreath makes an impressive decoration for a buffet table.

To make a rim of herbs on a glass, dip the rim of the glass in water and then in finely chopped fresh herbs.

The other garnishing suggestions shown are recommended for cheese or salad platters.

66

BUTTER

There are many attractive ways to serve butter. The whimsical butter dish illustrated above would be effective on a festive buffet table. To create it, place a slab of butter on an attractive plate. Decorate with butter shavings, butter balls, and radish slices. Garnish with a sprig of parsley.

Instructions for making the butter decorations shown on the facing page appear on pages 68 and 69.

The octagonal glass bowl of butter decorated with butter shavings and butter curls is a pleasing centerpiece for the Sunday breakfast table.
The butter tower, the butter grapes, or the butter rose could be used to embellish a cheese platter.
Butter balls rolled in herbs and spices and the herb butter slices laid out in an alternating pattern could be used for an informal buffet.

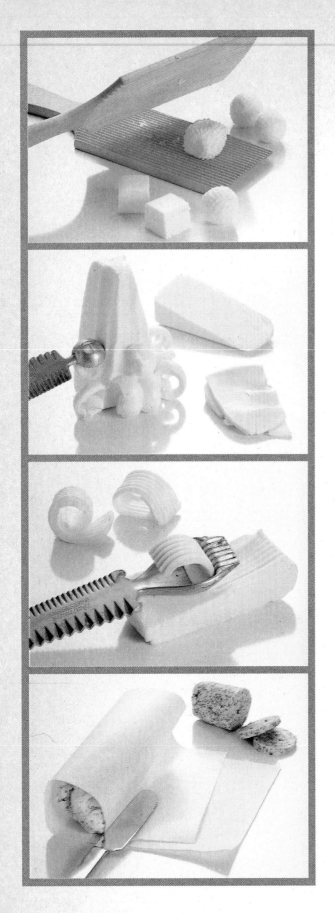

To make butter balls, cut a piece of butter into cubes. Roll the cubes into balls between two wet, rippled butter paddles.

To make a butter tower, cut a slab of butter into a cone shape. Use a butter scoop to carve rolls from top to bottom.

To make butter curls, run a ridged butter scraper on a slab of butter.

To make herb butter, mix softened butter with finely chopped fresh herbs such as parsley or chives. Wrap the mixture in a piece of waxed paper and, using a dull knife, shape it into a roll. Refrigerate until cold, then slice.

To make a butter rose, cut thin slices from a slab of slightly softened butter. Roll the first slice to make the center of the flower.

Place the other slices around the center of the flower. Arrange the outside petals so they touch and resemble a rose. Cut leaves from a slice of butter and decorate the rose. Refrigerate until ready to use.

To create an unusual butter dish, soften enough butter to fill an attractive glass bowl. After the bowl is filled, put it into the refrigerator so the butter will harden. Decorate with butter shavings and curls as shown.

Attractive butter balls can be made by rolling prepared balls in paprika and finely chopped parsley or chives.

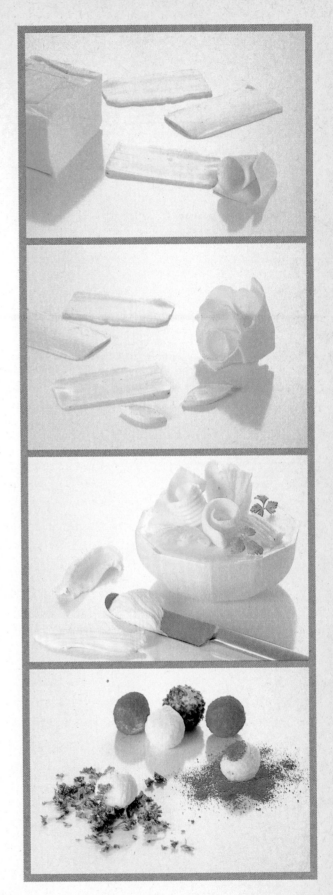

ASPICS AND GELATINS

A slice of cold meat decorated with fresh parsley, molded aspic, and aspic cubes, as illustrated above, may be served as an appetizer with a spicy mustard sauce.

To prepare aspic, mix 2 cups of beef broth with 2 egg whites in a medium-sized saucepan. Bring to a boil over high heat, and cook, stirring constantly, until the egg white coagulates. Strain the broth through cheesecloth so that it becomes clear. Stir in 1 tablespoon of plain gelatin that has been dissolved in 3 tablespoons of hot water. Pour the liquid into a large, very shallow pan and let cool. To remove the aspic after it has jelled, quickly dip the pan in hot water. Use a knife to free the aspic from the edge of the pan. Put a large plate or board on top of the pan and turn over quickly. The aspic is now ready to be cut into various attractive shapes.

Colorful garnishes can also be created from different flavors of gelatin. Those shown on the facing page were prepared according to the instructions on the package, and then, after cooling and setting in shallow pans, were cut like aspic.

Use savory aspic garnishes to decorate platters of ham and other meats. Shapes made from sweet gelatin may be used to embellish desserts.

To make green gelatin for decorative purposes, prepare lime gelatin according to the instructions on the package. Pour into a shallow pan, and let cool.

To remove the gelatin from the pan, quickly dip the pan in warm water. Put a plate or a board on top and quickly invert. Cut the gelatin into strips and then into small cubes.

Another way to make gelatin decorations is to pour the liquid gelatin into small bowls or molds and let cool.

To make red gelatin biscuits, turn out jelled cherry-flavored gelatin onto a wet plate. Use small cookie cutters to press out various designs.

To make a flower, pour cherry and lime gelatin into small bowls or molds. When the gelatin is set, turn it out and cut into quarters. Arrange the quarters in an alternating pattern.

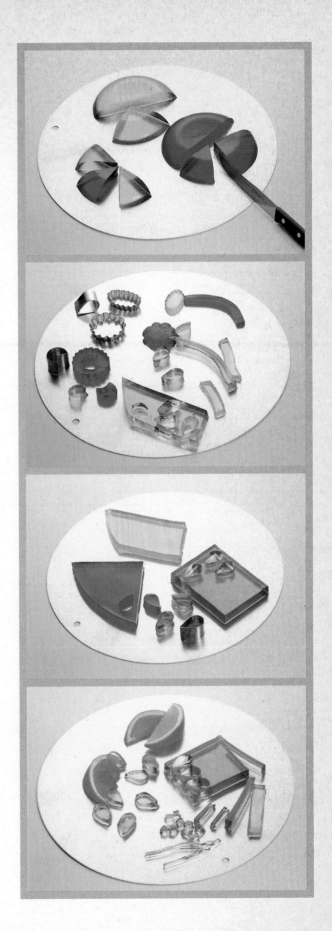

Gelatin cut with a variety of cookie cutters can be arranged in attractive patterns.

Use cookie cutters to press out garnishes in the shape of drops from different colored gelatin. Use to decorate desserts and fruit dishes.

Aspic can be prepared from any type of broth with the addition of plain gelatin. Use the proportions of broth to gelatin given on page 71. Pour the liquid aspic into several different molds, let set, turn it out, cut into shapes, and use for garnishing main-course dishes.

MEAT AND POULTRY PLATTER

MEAT PLATTER

COLD MEAT PLATTER

FISH PLATTER

CHEESE

Even a simple soft cheese can be garnished, as illustrated above. Place a round soft cheese on an attractive serving dish. Garnish with rosettes of farmer's cheese and a cherry tomato. Cut triangles from a slice of an Edam cheese. Press out rounds from thin cheese slices using a scallop-edged cookie cutter. Decorate the cheese with the cheese triangles and rounds.

On the facing page there are many ideas for cheese garnishes.

A thick slice of cheese can be cut into sticks and rolled in paprika.
Two different sizes of scallop-edged cookie cutters are used to press out cheese rounds. The smaller round is then stacked on the larger and garnished with stuffed olive slices.
Cut wedges of soft cheese, sprinkle with finely chopped chives, then tie with whole fresh chives.
Cut triangles from slices of cheese and arrange them in an appealing pattern.
Garnish cherry tomatoes with farmer's cheese or cream cheese mixed with horseradish.
Use colorful cocktail sticks to make kebabs of cherries, grapes, and tangerine segments with bite-sized cubes of cheese.

GLAZED FRUIT AND FLOWERS

An assortment of glazed fruit, illustrated above, makes an unusual decoration for desserts. When glazing fruit, all the fruit must be thoroughly washed and dried and at room temperature. To make the glaze, combine ½ cup sugar, ¾ cup water, and ⅛ teaspoon cream of tartar in a medium saucepan. Stirring constantly over low heat, bring the mixture to the hard ball stage. Remove the pan from the heat. Cool the glaze very slightly, then dip the fruit into it. Remove the fruit and set it on a wire rack to cool. Dust the fruit with super fine sugar. You can glaze an attractive assortment of fruit—for example, a selection of red, black, or purple grapes, cherries, raspberries, and strawberries.

Glazed flowers and leaves, illustrated on the facing page and prepared in the same way as the glazed fruit, make particularly lovely table decorations for such special occasions as engagement parties and weddings.

CANDIED FRUIT

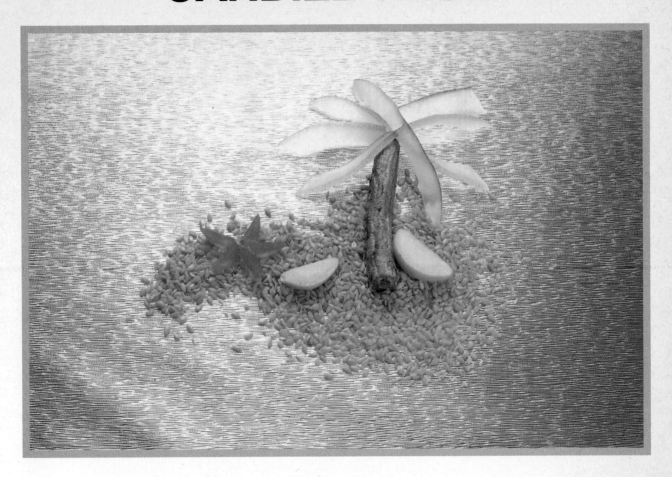

Many garnishes can be made from candied and dried fruits and nuts. The palm tree, shown above, has been created from a dried banana used to form the trunk. The palm leaves are fashioned from citron. Toasted sesame seeds are used for sand. The flower is made with a sliced candied cherry, and the stones from sliced Brazil nuts.

Garnishing ideas using candied fruit are illustrated on the facing page.

A lovely flower suitable for decorating a cake may be formed from candied lemon peel cut into strips, candied orange slices, candied pineapple pieces, and a green candied cherry.
Prunes decorated with almonds and dried banana slices as well as dates stuffed with cashew nuts make tasty decorations for roasted meat dishes.
The other garnishes shown make charming embellishments for ice cream or decorations for cakes and cookies.

MARZIPAN

On these pages there are instructions for making the marzipan decorations shown on pages 90 and 91. To prepare marzipan for decorating, knead 7 ounces marzipan dough (available in specialty food stores) with ½ cup confectioner's sugar.

To make a heart, roll marzipan out into a thick layer and press out a small heart with a cookie cutter. To make a hard chocolate icing, beat 1 large egg white until stiff. Gradually add 1½ cups confectioner's sugar and ½ cup baking cocoa and mix well. Put the icing into a pastry bag with a narrow, smooth tip. Decorate the heart with icing as shown, and add silver dragees.

To make letters, roll marzipan out into a thick layer, cut into strips, and shape into letters. Decorate the edge of each letter with chocolate icing as shown.

To make a mouse, shape the body and ears out of marzipan. Knead 1 to 2 tablespoons of baking cocoa into a small ball of marzipan, and use this to make the eyes, nose, and tail. Pinch the parts together to form the mouse.

To make the grass and flowers, knead a few drops of green food coloring into a small ball of marzipan. Roll it out to form a thin circle. Use your hands to shape it as you like. Make a few little green marzipan balls. Press out some light marzipan ovals with a scallop-edged cookie cutter. On one side of each oval, make a cut into the middle as shown. Arrange the cut ends so they overlap on top of each other in the shape of a flower. Put a green marzipan ball in the center of each flower. Decorate the grass with the marzipan flowers and personalize it with an inscription in confectioner's sugar icing. (For the icing, use the hard icing recipe from step 1, omitting the cocoa powder.)

To make a marzipan rose, knead a ball of marzipan with a few drops of red food coloring. Shape into small rounds with your thumb. Arrange the petals to form a rose. To make the leaves, knead a ball of marzipan with a few drops of green food coloring. Shape into rose leaves. Score the leaves with a knife in the pattern shown. Cut a stem from marzipan dough. Arrange the parts together to create a lovely rose.

To make pinwheels, knead a few drops of food coloring into two separate batches of marzipan, one red and one yellow. Knead one ball of natural marzipan. On a pastry board, roll the balls into three slabs of equal size. Trim the edges evenly with a knife. Lay the slabs on top of each other, roll them together, and cut into slices as shown.

To make a wreath, knead a few drops of green food coloring into a small ball of marzipan and with the palms of your hands shape it into a long, slender roll. Shape light marzipan into another roll in the same way. Intertwine the two rolls and arrange to form a wreath. Make green marzipan into small leaves. Pinch the leaves to the wreath. Add a few marzipan balls to create a flower.

To make a large flower basket, knead a few drops of red food coloring into a ball of marzipan and roll out the dough into a circle. Place a small glass bowl on top of it and press down. Be careful not to punch through the dough. Turn the edges up slightly to form a basket and remove the bowl. Put other marzipan decorations, such as the heart shown, inside the basket.

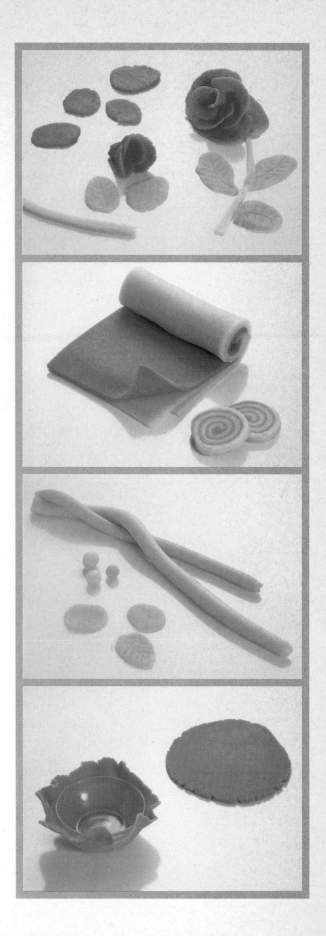

CHOCOLATE

Although it's unconventional, vegetables such as asparagus stalks, zucchini slices, and cocktail tomatoes can be dipped into melted chocolate, as can herbs like rosemary. These make unusual garnishes, as illustrated above.

Assorted fruits, shown on the facing page, include grapes, orange slices, peeled apples, pear quarters, strawberries, cooked rhubarb stalks, candied fruit, nuts, and leaves dipped in melted chocolate or brushed with chocolate. Instructions for coating fruit with chocolate and making chocolate decorations are given on pages 98 and 99.
Chocolate fruit makes a decorative addition to a dessert. Served with a vanilla or fruit sauce, chocolate-dipped fruit is also an elegant dessert by itself.

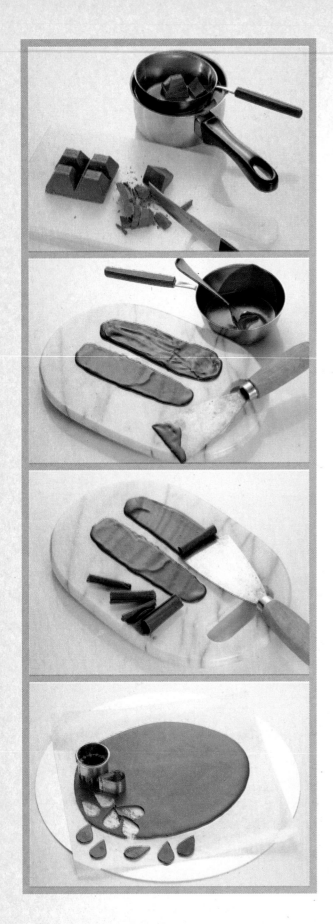

To melt chocolate, break a large bar of sweet German baking chocolate into chunks. Melt in the top of a double boiler over barely simmering water, stirring occasionally.

To make chocolate rolls, using a spoon or spatula, spread the melted chocolate onto a marble or porcelain slab as shown and let cool slightly.

Use the spatula to loosen and roll the cooled chocolate, as shown.

To make leaves, flowers, and other shapes, spread melted chocolate on a piece of baking parchment on a flat surface. Let the chocolate cool, then press out different shapes with small cookie cutters.

To make chocolate motifs, first make a parchment bag. Cut a triangle out of baking parchment. Twist to make a cone as shown and fold a little over the open ends so that the cone will hold together.

Fill the parchment bag with warm melted chocolate. Cut the tip off the point of the bag and create chocolate designs on another sheet of baking parchment. When the chocolate is completely cool, the motifs can be removed with a spatula and used to decorate cakes.

To make chocolate-covered fruit, dip a selection of fruit that is washed, dried, and at room temperature into melted chocolate. Cool on a wire rack. Ornamental leaves can be coated the same way. The actual leaves can be peeled away once the chocolate has hardened.

To make chocolate baskets, place a piece of plastic wrap over the bottoms of small glass bowls. Spread on melted chocolate. Let cool. Lift the chocolate-wrap from the bowl. Carefully remove the wrap from the chocolate.

THE ART
OF THE PASTRY TUBE

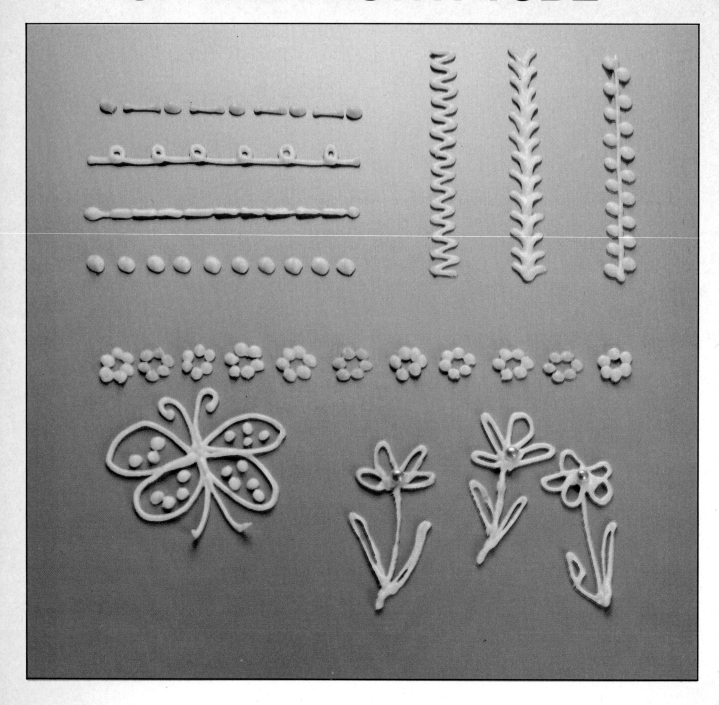

Beautiful decorations can be made from hard sugar icing, as illustrated on the facing page.

To make a hard sugar icing, you'll need 1½ cups confectioner's sugar and 1 large egg white. (Double the recipe depending on amount of icing needed.) Beat the egg white until stiff, gradually add the sugar, and stir until the icing forms. Divide into several batches and add a few drops of food coloring to make different colored icings. Put the icing into a pastry bag or baking parchment cone with a smooth, narrow tip. Use to decorate cookies and cakes.

Examples of butter cream and meringue decorations made with a pastry tube are shown on pages 102 and 103.

The butter cream designs were created by using a pastry tube with a smooth tip. Holding the pastry tube upright, squeeze out leaves, loops, and wavy lines.

To make the meringue batter, beat 1 large egg white until stiff, then gradually mix in ¼ cup sugar and ⅛ teaspoon cream of tarter. Spoon the meringue batter into a pastry tube with a jagged tip. Line a cookie sheet with baking parchment. Holding the tube at an angle, squeeze out wavy lines, rosettes, and other imaginative designs.
Bake for one hour on the bottom rack of a preheated oven at 225°F. Let cool for about five minutes before removing the meringues from the cookie sheet.

DESSERTS

To create the dish of fruit purees shown on page 104, puree a kiwi. Then puree several large strawberries. Arrange the purees on a plate as shown.

Next, puree a peeled, pitted peach. Then puree ⅓ cup of blueberries. Add to the other fruit purees as shown.

Use a thin wooden stick to swirl the fruit purees into each other.

To caramelize sugar for garnishes, melt 1 cup of sugar in a heavy saucepan over very low heat. Stirring occasionally, this should take 8 to 10 minutes. Very carefully pour the caramel onto a heat-proof plate or marble slab. Pull out fine threads with a spoon.

To make a sugar rim on glasses, dip the rims first in egg white and then in confectioner's sugar.

To decorate a glass as shown on page 104, first make a cut into the middle of a small paper doily.

Glue the doily to the stem of the glass (make sure to use a water-soluble glue). Fill the glass with Strawberry Whipped Cream (see recipe page 108). Decorate with rosettes of whipped cream.

Tie a bright pink ribbon around the stem of the glass.

DOUBLE CREAM PUDDING
(See photograph on page 104, upper left)

Vanilla cream ingredients
- 1 package vanilla pudding mix
- 1⅔ cups cold milk
- ⅓ cup sour cream

Lemon cream ingredients
- 1 package lemon pudding mix
- 2 egg yolks
- ½ cup sugar
- 2¼ cups water
- ⅓ cup yogurt

Prepare each pudding separately. To make the vanilla cream, in a medium saucepan, mix the pudding powder into the milk. Bring to a boil over medium heat, stirring frequently. Cool slightly, then stir in the sour cream. Set aside. To make the lemon cream, in a medium saucepan, combine ¼ cup of water with the sugar, egg yolks, and pudding mix. Add the remaining water (2 cups) and bring to a boil. Cool slightly and stir in the yogurt. Layer the two creams equally in eight glasses with sugared rims. Garnish with glazed red currants.

STRAWBERRY WHIPPED CREAM
(See photograph on pages 104 and 105, upper center)

Ingredients
- 1 package strawberry mousse or pudding mix
- ½ cup cold milk
- ½ cup heavy cream
- 2 tablespoons raspberry brandy

Prepare the mousse by beating the mix with the milk in the bowl of an electric mixer set at high speed for 3 to 5 minutes; or according to the instructions on the package. Beat the cream until stiff, mix in the raspberry brandy. Setting aside ¼ of the whipped cream, gently fold the rest into the mousse; spoon into four glasses. Use the remaining cream to form decorative rosettes (from a pastry tube) on each pudding.

CRÈME CARAMEL
(See photograph on page 105)

Ingredients
- 3 eggs plus 3 additional egg yolks
- ½ cup sugar
- 1 teaspoon vanilla extract
- 1 cup milk
- 1 cup heavy cream

Preheat oven to 300° F. In the bowl of an electric mixer, beat eggs and egg yolks together until foamy. Blend in sugar and vanilla, add milk and heavy cream. Spoon the custard into four heat-proof molds placed in a baking pan filled with water. Bake for 50 minutes.

Let the custard cool thoroughly, then carefully turn out onto serving plates. When completely cool, refrigerate until serving. Garnish with walnuts, caramelized sugar (see step 4, page 106), and chocolate leaves. Top with rosettes of whipped cream.

TRIPLE FRUIT PUREE
(See photograph on page 104, lower left)

Ingredients
1 14-ounce can of apricots
1 tablespoon apricot brandy
1 pint fresh or frozen raspberries
1 tablespoon sugar

1 tablespoon raspberry brandy
3 kiwis
1 tablespoon orange liqueur
4 tablespoons blackberry jam

Drain the apricots and puree them in a food processor or blender. Mix in the apricot brandy. Pour into a small bowl and set aside.

Pick over the raspberries, wash them, then puree them in a food processor or blender. Mix in the sugar and raspberry brandy and set aside in a small bowl.

Peel the kiwis, then puree them in the food processor or blender. Mix in the orange liqueur. Spoon equal portions of each of the three fruit purees onto four dessert plates. Put a tablespoon of jam in the middle of each portion. Stir the jam slightly through the purees using a thin wooden stick. Garnish with mint leaves and halved strawberries.

TROPICAL GELATIN
(Not illustrated)

Ingredients
1 package mixed fruit gelatin
1 cup boiling water

1 cup cold water
1 mango, cut into strips

In a medium-sized bowl, dissolve the gelatin powder together with the boiling water. Add the cold water. Pour into four attractive individual molds. Put the molds in the refrigerator until the gelatin sets. To remove the gelatin from the molds, dip them quickly into hot water, then turn out onto dessert plates. Garnish with whipped cream and mango strips.

COOKIE
FLOWER BASKET

To make the flower basket illustrated on pages 112 and 113, first prepare and roll out the dough, following the recipe on page 116. Then, draw a paper pattern for the basket as shown. (The basket should be just about as tall as the width of your baking sheet.) Cut it out.

Place the rolled-out dough on a greased cookie sheet. Put the pattern on top.

Cut out the design using a sharp paring knife. Reserve the scraps of dough.

Using the palms of your hands, shape the remaining dough into three thin rolls the width of the basket, five thin rolls the height of the basket, and two very thin rolls that extend from one edge to the other and slightly beyond. Intertwine the two long, very thin rolls.

Weave the thicker rolls on top of the cut-out dough to create a basket pattern. Arrange the intertwined roll as shown.

Brush the basket with milk or beaten egg white. Following the photograph on pages 112 and 113, create flowers with raisins, halved almonds, pistachios, sunflower seeds, pumpkin seeds, and sesame seeds. Sprinkle with 1 teaspoon of unrefined sugar crystals. Bake in a pre-heated 350° F oven for about 25 minutes.

To make the cookies shown on pages 110 and 111, use the recipes for cookie dough on pages 116 and 117. Roll the dough out thinly on a pastry board or marble slab and press out an assortment of designs with cookie cutters.

Make a hard sugar icing using 1½ cups confectioner's sugar and 1 large egg white. Beat the egg white until stiff, add the sugar, and stir until the icing forms. Divide into several batches and add a few drops of food coloring to make pink and yellow icings. Spread the icing on the cookies and decorate with colored dragees and small candies as shown.

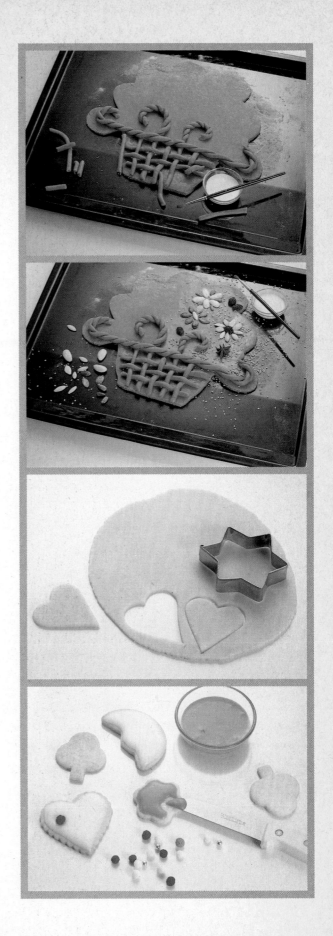

COOKIE FLOWER BASKET
(See photograph on pages 112 and 113)

Ingredients

1 cup honey

⅓ cup sugar

1 teaspoon vanilla extract

2 eggs

2 tablespoons softened margarine

4 cups plus 3 tablespoons flour

1 teaspoon cinnamon

¼ cup baking cocoa

2½ teaspoons baking powder

Combine the honey, sugar, vanilla, eggs, and margarine in the bowl of an electric mixer and beat well. Sift the flour, cinnamon, cocoa, and baking powder together, and gradually add to the batter. You may have to knead in the last cup of flour by hand.

Knead the dough on a pastry board dusted with flour; roll out the dough to a thickness of ½ inch. Follow the directions given on pages 114 and 115 for finishing the cookie flower basket.

The cookies shown on pages 110 and 111 can be made from different types of cookie dough. Three basic recipes for cookie dough are given on these pages.

COOKIE DOUGH I—BUTTER COOKIES
(See photograph on pages 110 and 111)

Ingredients

2 cups + 1 tablespoon flour

1 teaspoon baking powder

¼ teaspoon salt

⅓ cup sugar

1 teaspoon vanilla extract

1 egg

1 tablespoon milk

½ cup softened sweet butter or margarine

Preheat oven to 350°F. Sift together the flour, baking powder, and salt. Combine the sugar, vanilla extract, egg, milk, and shortening in the bowl of an electric mixer and beat well. Gradually add the flour mixture. Turn out onto a floured pastry board and knead to make a smooth dough. If the dough is too sticky to handle, refrigerate it for about 30 minutes.

Roll the dough out thinly. Press out the cookies using assorted cookie cutters.

Place the cookies on a lightly greased baking sheet. Bake for about 10 minutes. Cool briefly, then remove the cookies from the pan, and set them on a wire rack. When the cookies are thoroughly cool, decorate them with icing and small candies.

COOKIE DOUGH II—LEMON COOKIES

(See photogragh on pages 110 and 111)

Ingredients

2 egg yolks
1 cup sifted confectioner's sugar
¼ teaspoon salt

1 teaspoon lemon extract
1 teaspoon grated lemon peel
2½ cups flour

Preheat oven to 350° F. Beat egg yolks in the bowl of an electric mixer until they are foamy, gradually mix in the sugar. Add the salt, lemon extract, and lemon peel and mix well. Beat in the flour a little at a time. Turn the dough onto a floured pastry board and knead until it is smooth. If the dough is too sticky to handle, refrigerate it for about 30 minutes.

Roll out the dough thinly. Press out various shapes with a selection of cookie cutters.

Place the cookies on a lightly greased baking sheet. Bake for 8 to 10 minutes. Remove from oven and let the cookies cool briefly. Remove to a wire rack. Ice and decorate with icing when they are no longer warm to the touch.

COOKIE DOUGH III—HONEY-SPICE COOKIES

(See photograph on pages 110 and 111)

Ingredients

1 cup honey
½ cup sugar
1 teaspoon vanilla extract
3 drops lemon extract
1 egg
4 cups + 2 tablespoons flour
2½ teaspoons baking powder

1 tablespoon cinnamon
⅛ teaspoon cloves
⅛ teaspoon nutmeg
¼ cup milk
Almonds, raisins, candied cherries,
 and citron

Preheat oven to 350° F. In the bowl of an electric mixer, combine the honey, sugar, vanilla, lemon extract, and egg. Mix thoroughly. Sift together the flour, baking soda, cinnamon, cloves, and nutmeg. Gradually work the flour mixture into the batter until it forms a dough. Turn the dough out onto a floured pastry board and knead until smooth.

Roll the dough out to a thickness of ½ inch. Press out the cookies with cookie cutters. Place the cookies on a lightly greased baking pan. Brush the cookies with milk. Decorate with almonds, cherries, raisins, and citron.

Bake the cookies for about 25 minutes. When the cookies are slightly cool, put them on a wire rack to cool completely.

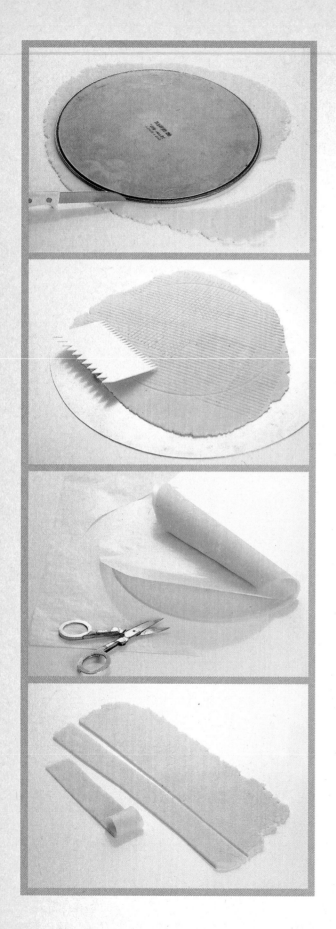

Decorating instructions follow for the marzipan cake recipe on page 126. To cover a cake with marzipan, first knead 14 ounces of marzipan (available in specialty food stores) together with 1 cup confectioner's sugar. Roll out the marzipan on a marble pastry slab sprinkled with confectioner's sugar. The marzipan must be slightly more than 9 inches in diameter or a little bit larger than the bottom of the cake pan you are using. Lay the bottom of the 9-inch springform pan, in which the cake was baked, on top of the marzipan and cut out a circle. Reserve the scraps of marzipan.

If you want to have a pattern on the marzipan like the cake on the bottom of page 118, follow the instructions in the previous step for preparing and rolling out the marzipan. Then use a fork or dough comb lengthwise and crosswise to create the pattern. Cut out the dough circle.

Cut out a round of baking parchment using the bottom of the springform pan as a pattern. Put the parchment on top of the marzipan circle, then roll them up together.

Roll out another ball of marzipan from the scraps. Cut out a strip to fit around the edge of the cake. Roll up and set aside.

Place the marzipan circle on the top of the cooled cake. Unroll and carefully press down.

Place the marzipan strip on the side of the cake. Unroll and carefully press down. Complete the decorations shown on page 118 by adding a bow of green marzipan, marzipan triangles and leaves, small sugared candies, and rosettes of whipped cream.

When you ice a cake such as the German Wreath (see the recipe given on pages 124 and 125), a piece of cardboard can be used to press toasted almond slices around it.

To decorate the French Chocolate Cake shown at the top of page 118 (see page 124 for the recipe), first ice the cake with 8 ounces of melted bittersweet chocolate. Using the recipe for hard sugar icing given on page 101, prepare a white hard sugar icing. Spoon it into a cone of baking parchment. (See page 99.) Squeeze out a spiral, starting in the middle of the cake, onto the wet chocolate icing. Take a pointed wooden stick and draw eight lines from the center of the cake to the edge as shown. Candied cherries add a finishing touch.

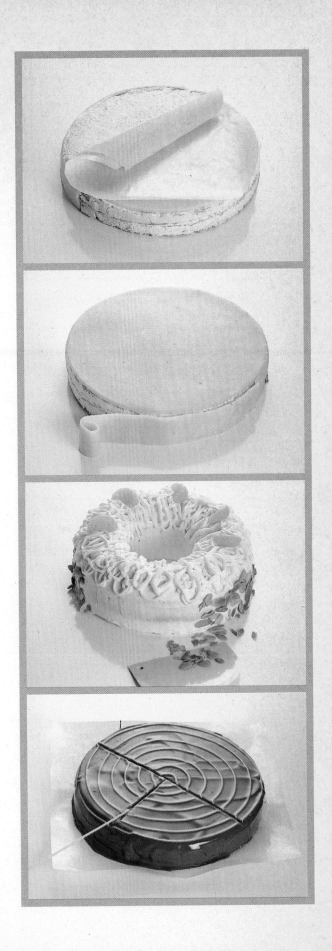

STENCIL DECORATIONS

A plain cake, iced with butter cream, can be made to look very special by simply stenciling a design on the top with confectioner's sugar on the top and sides. To make the design on the cake at the left, place a heart stencil on top. Using a small strainer, sift ¼ cup confectioner's sugar onto the top and sides of the cake. Carefully remove the stencil.

To make the design on the cake at the left, sift the top and sides of a sponge cake with confectioner's sugar. Place a flower stencil on top. Sift ¼ cup baking cocoa onto the top of the cake. Carefully remove the stencil.

Paper doilies make excellent stencils or you can draw your own stencil designs on pieces of paper and cut them out. Attach a strip of paper to each stencil to make it easy to remove from the cake.

To make the oblong cake shown at the left, first create triangular stencils as shown. Cover alternate areas and sift with cocoa powder using a small strainer. Cover up the cocoa-covered areas, then sprinkle with grated coconut.

FRENCH CHOCOLATE CAKE

(See photograph on page 118, upper left)

Ingredients

Cake

- 6 eggs
- 1 cup softened sweet butter or margarine
- 1 cup sugar
- 1 teaspoon vanilla extract
- 2 cups plus 2 tablespoons flour
- 2 teaspoons baking powder
- 8 ounces bittersweet baking chocolate, grated
- ½ cup ground almonds

Icing

- 1 cup brandy or rum
- 2 to 3 tablespoons apricot jam
- 8 ounces bittersweet chocolate
- 1½ cups confectioner's sugar
- 1 egg white

Preheat oven to 350° F. In the bowl of an electric mixer, combine the eggs, butter or margarine, sugar, and vanilla. Beat until smooth. Sift the flour with the baking powder, and gradually beat into the batter. Combine the grated chocolate with the ground almonds, and mix in one tablespoon at a time, by hand. Turn the dough into a greased 9-inch springform baking pan, and bake for about 1 hour.

Remove the cake from the oven. Put the pan on a wire rack and pour the brandy or rum over the cake. Let cool. When the cake is completely cool, remove from the baking pan.

In a small saucepan, combine the jam with 1 tablespoon of water and melt over low heat. Spread the liquid jam on the top of the cake.

Melt chocolate for the icing in the top of a double boiler over simmering water. Spread the icing over the top and sides of the cake. While the icing is still wet, prepare the hard sugar icing according to the recipe given on page 101. Using a baking parchment cone, squeeze out a spiral of white icing as shown on page 121, starting from the center of the cake. While the icing is still wet, draw eight lines at equal intervals from the center of the cake to the edge. Divide these eight lines in two to make a total of sixteen lines. Let the icing harden.

GERMAN WREATH

(See photograph on pages 118 and 119, top center)

Ingredients

Cake

- 7 tablespoons softened sweet butter or margarine
- ¾ cup sugar
- 1 teaspoon vanilla extract
- 1 teaspoon rum
- 3 eggs
- 7 tablespoons cornstarch
- 2 teaspoons baking powder

Filling and Icing

- 1 package vanilla pudding mix
- 2 cups cold milk
- 1 cup softened sweet butter
- 3 tablespoons raspberry jam
- 1 cup toasted almond slices
- 1 tangerine

Preheat oven to 325° F. Cream the butter or margarine in the bowl of an electric mixer. Beat in the sugar a little at a time. Add the vanilla and the rum. Beat in one egg at a time. Beat each egg for 1 minute. Sift the cornstarch with the baking powder and stir into the batter. Turn the dough into a greased ring mold or tube pan. Bake for 35 to 40 minutes.

To make the filling, combine the pudding mix with the milk in a small saucepan. Bring to a boil, stirring frequently. Cool slightly. Carefully stir in the softened butter 1 tablespoon at a time. Caution: if either the pudding or butter are too cold, the icing will curdle.

Slice the ring into two layers. Spread raspberry jam on the bottom layer. Spread a little butter cream on top. Put all the layers together. Frost the ring with the remaining butter cream and decorate with toasted almond slices and tangerine segments as illustrated. (See step 8, page 121 for additional photograph.)

VANILLA CREAM CAKE
(See photograph on page 119, upper right)

Ingredients
Cake

3 eggs
¾ cup sugar
1 teaspoon vanilla extract
¾ cup plus 1 tablespoon flour
¾ cup plus 1 tablespoon cornstarch
3 teaspoons baking powder

Filling and Icing

1 package vanilla pudding mix
2 cups cold milk
1 cup softened sweet butter, at room temperature
3 tablespoons apricot jam
8 ounces bittersweet chocolate
chocolate sprinkles
⅛ cup red jellybeans

Preheat oven to 350° F. Line the bottom of a 9-inch springform pan with baking parchment. Grease the parchment and the sides of the pan. Separate the eggs, being careful not to mix the white with the yolk. In the bowl of an electric mixer, beat the egg yolks with 3 tablespoons of warm water. Gradually add ½ cup of the sugar and the vanilla, and mix until creamy. In a separate bowl, beat the egg whites until they are stiff. Gradually beat in the remaining sugar. Gently fold (do not stir) the egg whites into the batter. Sift the flour with the cornstarch and baking powder. Gently fold (do not stir) into the batter. Turn the batter into the springform baking pan. Bake for 20 to 30 minutes. Put the pan on a wire rack and allow the cake to cool completely.

When the cake is cool, make the filling. Combine the pudding mix with the milk in a small saucepan, and bring to a boil, stirring frequently. Cool slightly. Carefully stir in the softened butter 1 tablespoon at a time. Caution: if either the pudding or butter are too cold, the icing will curdle.

Cut the cake crosswise to make three layers. Melt the chocolate in the top of a double boiler over simmering water. Cover the top of one layer with melted chocolate, then cover the chocolate with a little butter cream. Place the second layer on top of the first, and cover the top with apricot jam. Cover the jam with a little butter cream. Place the top layer on the cake, and thinly ice the top and sides of the cake with butter cream. Using a piece of cardboard, press chocolate sprinkles around the side of the cake. Put the remaining butter cream into a pastry tube and pipe out rosettes and edging as shown. Decorate with red jellybeans.

MARZIPAN CAKE
(See photograph on page 118, lower left)

Ingredients
Cake
5 eggs

1 cup softened sweet butter or margarine

1 cup sugar

1 teaspoon vanilla extract

2 cups plus 2 tablespoons flour

2 teaspoons baking powder

Filling
16 ounces softened cream cheese

3 teaspoons lemon extract

2 teaspoons grated lemon peel

2 cups heavy cream

⅓ cup sugar

2 teaspoons cream of tartar

4 tablespoons blackberry jam

Decorations
14 ounces prepared marzipan

1 cup confectioner's sugar

green food coloring

dragees

Preheat oven to 350° F. Line the bottom of a 9-inch springform pan with baking parchment. Grease the paper and the sides of the pan. In the bowl of an electric mixer beat the eggs until foamy. Gradually add in the sugar and vanilla. Sift the flour and baking powder together, and beat into the batter. Turn into the springform pan. Bake for 45 to 55 minutes. Allow the cake to cool on a wire rack. When it is completely cool, remove it from the pan.

Combine the cream cheese, lemon extract, and grated lemon peel and mix well. In a separate bowl, beat the heavy cream until stiff. Gradually beat in the sugar and cream of tartar.

Carefully fold the whipped cream into the cream cheese mixture; do not stir.

Slice the cake crosswise in thirds to make three layers. Spread 2 tablespoons of jam on the first layer. Spread one-third of the cream mixture over the jam. Put the middle layer on the top and spread first with the remaining jam and then with half the remaining cream. Place the upper layer on top and thinly cover the whole cake with the remaining cream.

Following the instructions given on pages 120 and 121, and the photograph on page 118, cover the cake with marzipan and decorate it.

CHOCOLATE PUDDING CAKE
(See photograph on pages 118 and 119, lower center)

Ingredients
Cake
2 eggs

1 tablespoon warm water

⅓ plus 2 tablespoons sugar

1 teaspoon vanilla extract

⅔ cup flour

7 tablespoons cornstarch

1 teaspoon baking powder

3½ tablespoons melted sweet butter or margarine

Filling and Icing

1 package chocolate pudding mix
2 cups cold milk
1 cup softened sweet butter, at room temperature

4 ounces bittersweet chocolate, shaved
sweetened whipped cream
chocolate ornaments

Preheat oven to 350° F. Line the bottom of an oblong cake pan with baking parchment. Grease the paper and the sides of the pan. In the bowl of an electric mixer, beat the eggs and water until the mixture is creamy. Gradually add the sugar and vanilla and mix well. Sift the flour, cornstarch, and baking powder together, and fold into the batter. Do not stir. Fold in the melted butter. Do not stir. Turn the batter into the prepared pan. Bake for about 30 minutes. Cool the cake thoroughly on a wire rack.

To make the filling, combine the pudding mix with the milk in a small saucepan. Bring to a boil, stirring frequently. Remove from heat and cool slightly. Carefully stir in the softened butter 1 tablespoon at a time. Caution: if either the pudding or butter are too cold, the icing will curdle.

Cut the cake in half crosswise to form two layers. Spread the lower layer with one-third of the butter cream. Place the upper layer on top and ice the top and sides with the remaining butter cream. Press the chocolate shavings around the sides of the cake. Decorate with rosettes of whipped cream and chocolate ornaments as shown.

PINEAPPLE MERINGUE TARTS
(See photograph on page 119, bottom right)

Buy or bake several small shortbread cakes or plain tarts. Place a pineapple ring on top of each one. Decorate with meringue from a pastry tube, using the meringue recipe and instructions on pages 101 to 103. Put the tarts under the broiler for 2 to 3 minutes or until the meringue turns golden brown. Cool slightly before serving.

FESTIVE MOCHA CREAM CAKE
(See photograph of the cake decorated with hearts on page 122, top)

Ingredients

Cake
2 eggs
2 tablespoons hot water
⅓ cup + 2 tablespoons sugar
1 teaspoon vanilla extract
⅔ cup flour
7 tablespoons cornstarch
1 teaspoon baking powder

Filling and Icing
2 cups cold milk
2 teaspoons instant espresso coffee
1 tablespoon coffee liqueur
1 package chocolate pudding mix
1 cup softened sweet butter
½ cup baking cocoa
½ cup confectioner's sugar

Preheat the oven to 350° F. Line the bottom of a 9-inch springform pan with baking parchment. Grease the paper and the sides of the pan. Combine the eggs and water in the bowl of an electric mixer and beat until foamy or for at least 1 minute. Gradually mix in the sugar and vanilla, and beat for another 2 minutes. Sift the flour, cornstarch, and baking powder together. Sift half of the flour mixture into the batter; mix well, then sift in the other half. Stir lightly. Turn the batter into the prepared springform pan. Bake for 20 to 30 minutes. Cool thoroughly on a wire rack.

In a small saucepan over low heat dissolve the instant coffee in 3 tablespoons of the milk. Add the coffee liqueur. Stir in the remaining milk and pudding mix. Increase the heat and bring to a boil, stirring frequently. Cool slightly. Carefully stir in the softened butter 1 tablespoon at a time. Caution: if either the pudding or butter are too cold, the icing will curdle.

Cut the cake crosswise in thirds to make three layers. Spread one-third of the butter cream over the first layer, add the second layer. Spread one-third of the butter cream over the second layer, then add the top layer. Thinly ice the top and sides of the cake with the remaining butter cream. Follow the instructions given on page 123 for decorating a cake with a stencil, covering with sifted cocoa powder, and then with confectioner's sugar.

BLACK AND WHITE CAKE

(See photograph on page 122, bottom; see step 4 and photograph on page 123)

Ingredients

Cake

2 eggs

2 tablespoons hot water

⅓ cup sugar

1 teaspoon vanilla extract

½ cup flour

3½ tablespoons cornstarch

1 teaspoon baking powder

Filling and Icing

1 package vanilla pudding mix

2 cups cold milk

2 tablespoons rum

1 cup softened sweet butter, at room temperature

2 tablespoons apricot jam

¼ cup baking cocoa

¼ cup shredded coconut

Preheat oven to 350° F. Line the bottom and sides of an oblong baking pan with baking parchment, leaving a lip of paper above the sides of the pan. Grease the paper and the sides of the pan. Beat the eggs and water in the bowl of an electric mixer until foamy, about 1 minute. Mix in the sugar and vanilla, and beat for another 2 minutes. Sift the flour together with the cornstarch and baking powder. Sift half the flour mixture into the cake batter. Mix gently, then sift in the other half. Mix gently. Turn the batter into the prepared pan. Bake for 10 to 12 minutes.

Cool thoroughly on a wire rack and remove the baking parchment from the cake.

In a small saucepan, combine the pudding mix with the milk and the rum. Bring to a boil over medium heat, stirring frequently. Cool slightly. Carefully stir in the softened butter 1 tablespoon at a time. Caution: if either the pudding or butter are too cold, the icing will curdle.

Cut the cake crosswise in two layers. Spread the jam on the bottom half, then cover with a little butter cream. Put the upper layer on the cake and ice the top and sides with the remaining butter cream. Follow the instructions given for decorating a cake with stencils on page 123. Sift the cake with cocoa powder and sprinkle on shredded coconut.

BREAD BASKET
—for breakfast or a brunch buffet

VEGETABLE CENTERPIECE
—for a country-style buffet

FRUIT BOWL

—for a dessert buffet

Note: the rhubarb leaves and uncooked stalks shown in this photograph are not edible.

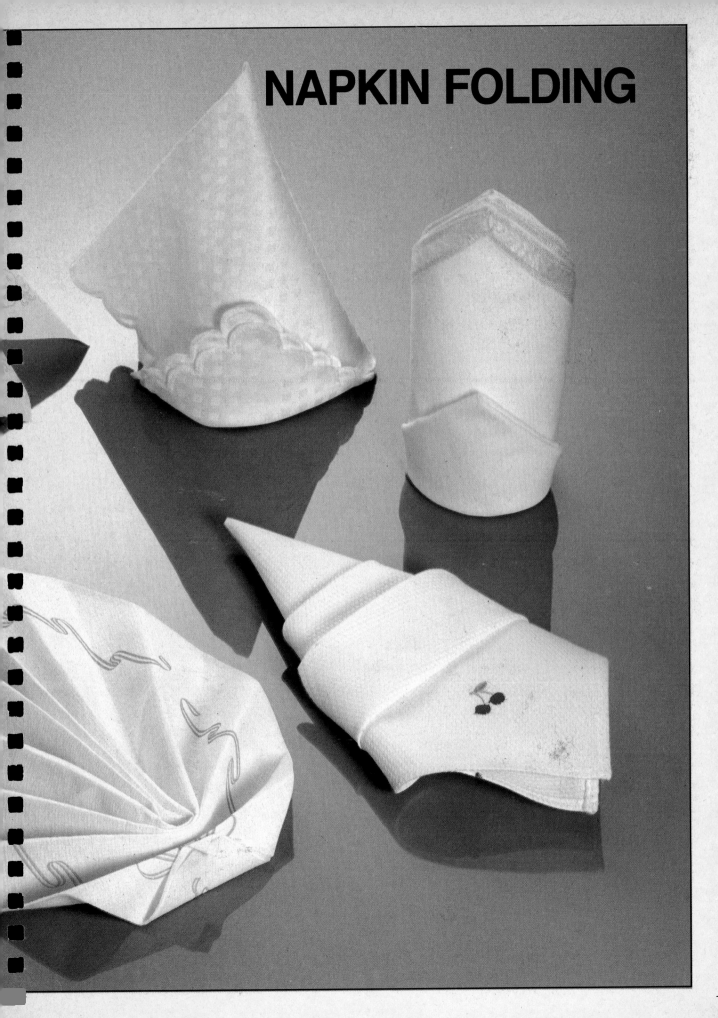

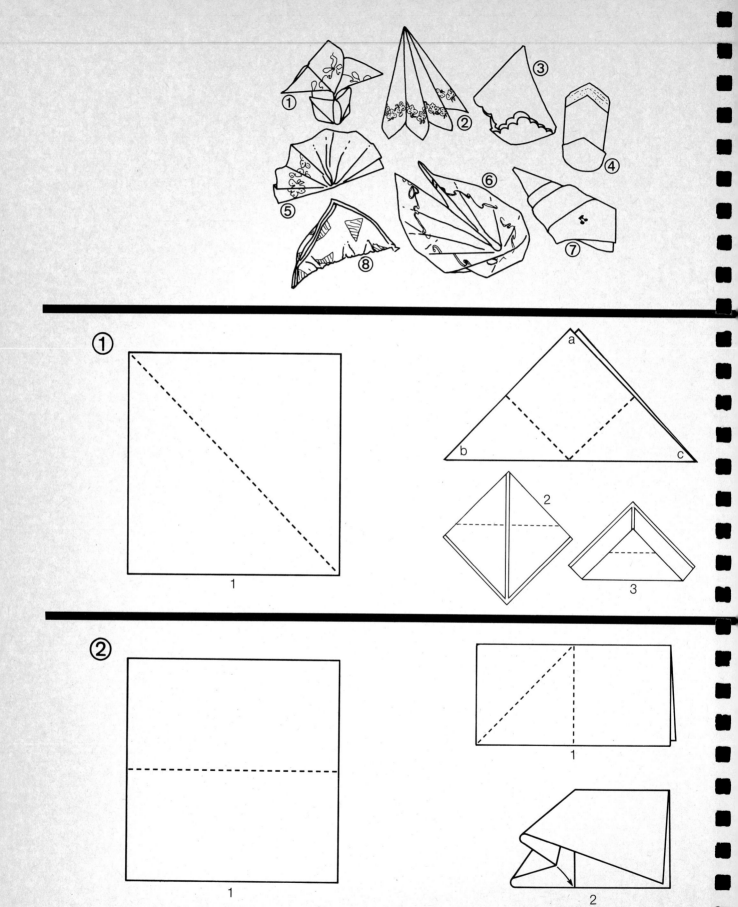

Attractively folded napkins enhance every table. Special napkins provide a gracious decoration for formal occasions, but they also look lovely on an elegantly set tea table, or at a children's party.
Formal or informal, a table setting is always incomplete without napkins.

The illustration on the left, photographed on pages 136 and 137, shows some of the different ways that linen and paper napkins may be folded.

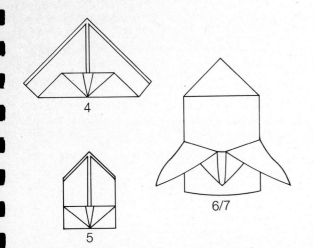

1. Fold a napkin into a triangle.
2. Fold corner b onto corner a. Fold corner c onto corner a, so that you create a square.
3. Fold the square about ¾ of an inch below the center line to form a triangle.
4. Fold back the point of the smaller triangle lying on the top so that the point touches the base of the triangle.
5. Fold the right and left corners back and tuck them into each other. Give the napkin a rounded shape; it will stand up better.
6. Carefully pull out the two upper front points.
7. The napkin is complete: a fleur-de-lis.

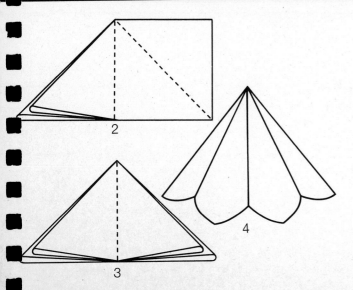

1. Fold the napkin in the middle to form an oblong, with the open part on the bottom.
2. Fold in the upper right-hand corner between the upper and lower napkin layers to form a triangle.
3. Repeat this step with the left side of the napkin.
4. Set up the napkin as shown.

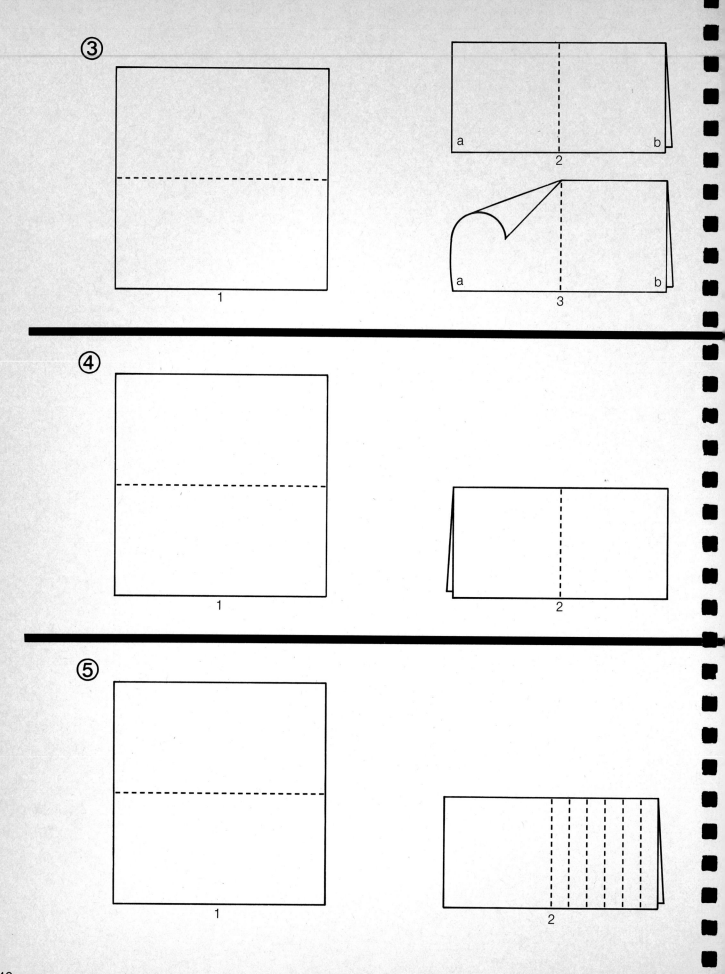

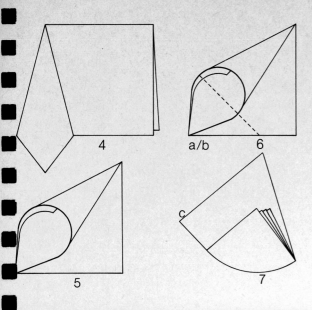

1. Fold the napkin in the middle to form an ob-long.
2. Mark the middle of the napkin.
3. Roll in the left half to the middle so it forms a cone.
4. Place corner a on corner b.
5. Fold the four points of corner a/b up and out.
6. Leave corner c exposed and free. Fluff out the napkin and set it up.
7. The finished napkin.

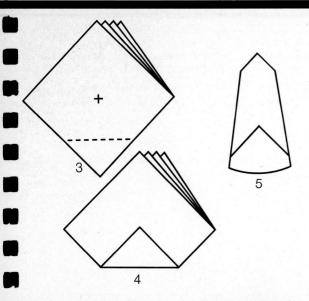

1. Fold the napkin in the middle to form an ob-long.
2. Fold the napkin again in the middle and make a square.
3. Turn the bottom corner of the square up into the middle.
4. Fold the side corners around the back and tuck them together.
5. The finished napkin.

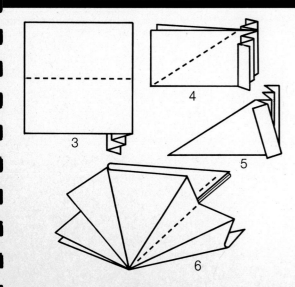

1. Fold the napkin in the middle to form an ob-long.
2. Beginning from the right, make an accordion-pleat fold in a little more than half the napkin.
3. Fold the napkin in the middle so that the open edges face up.
4. Fold down the top left corner at an angle to make a stand.
5. Fan out the accordion fold. The napkin will stand up by itself.
6. The finished napkin.

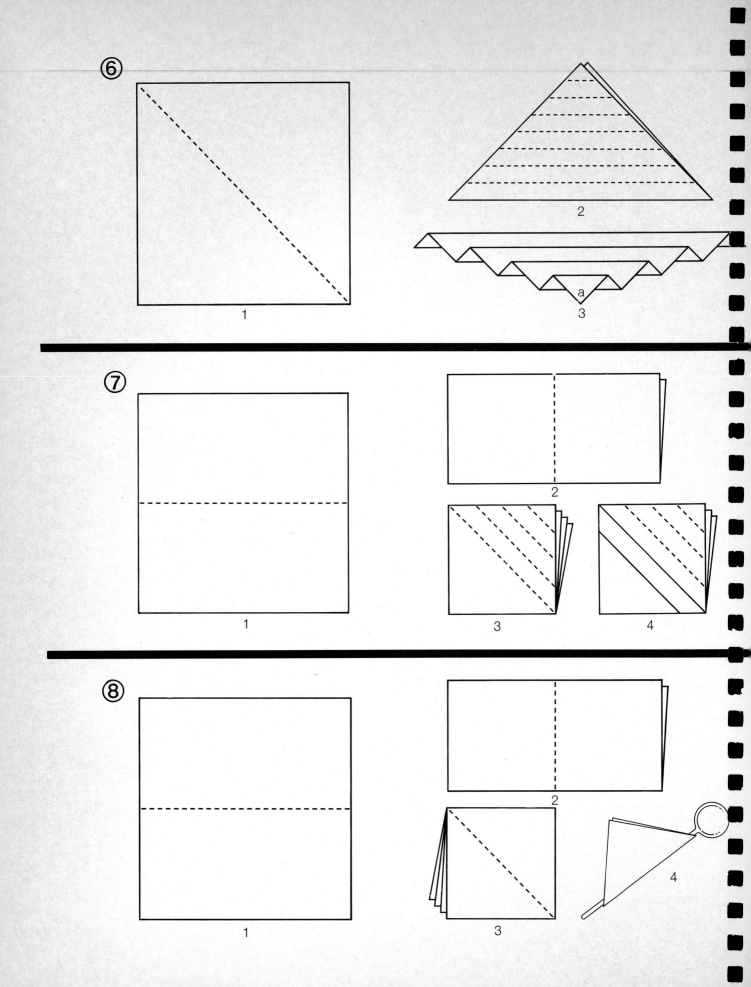

⑥

1

2

3

a

⑦

1

2

3

4

⑧

1

2

3

4

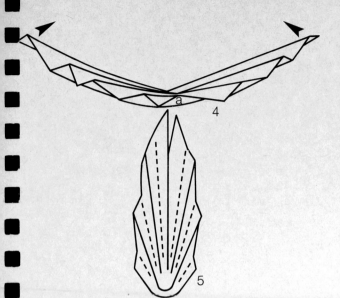

1. Fold a square napkin into a triangle.
2. Make horizontal accordion folds in the triangle, each about ¾ of an inch wide.
3. The napkin will now be shaped like a narrow ribbon. Place the side with point a on the bottom.
4. Pull one end over the center "a" and onto the other end.
5. The finished napkin.

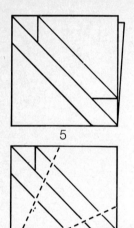

1. Fold the napkin in the middle to form an oblong.
2. Fold the napkin once again in the middle and make a square.
3. All the open sides should face toward the upper right. Fold the upper layer toward the middle four times; the fourth fold will form the main diagonal.
4. Fold the second napkin layer three times the same way; the edge of the strip should lie on the main diagonal.
5. Fold the third layer over the edge of the second layer, and slide under the first edge.
6. Fold the left and the lower sides around the back, so that they lie upon the diagonal.
7. The finished napkin.

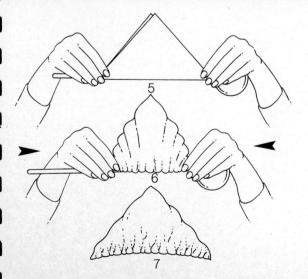

1. Fold the napkin in the middle to form an oblong.
2. Fold the napkin once again in the middle and make a square.
3. Fold the napkin once again to form a triangle.
4. Insert a spoon through the napkin.
5. Hold the ends of the napkin with your hands.
6. Squeeze the ends of the napkin together.
7. The finished napkin.